TO WHERE ARE WE BOUND

poems by

Benjamin Mueller

Finishing Line Press
Georgetown, Kentucky

TO WHERE ARE WE BOUND

Copyright © 2020 by Benjamin Mueller
ISBN 978-1-64662-167-5 First Edition
All rights reserved under International and Pan-American Copyright Conventions. No part of this book may be reproduced in any manner whatsoever without written permission from the publisher, except in the case of brief quotations embodied in critical articles and reviews.

ACKNOWLEDGMENTS

The following works were previously published:

"White Egret" in *Valparaiso Poetry Review*
"Upon Witnessing the Pelican's Dive" in *Split Rock Review*
"Colossus, PA" in *Washington Square Review*
"Tulip Tree" in *Euphony*
"To Mr. ___ for Accommodating his Customers with an Extra Parking Lot" in *Chronogram Magazine*
"To Fisheyes Who Collected Old Songs" and "To the Laundromat Attendant and Her Husband's Missing Sock" in *Two Hawks Quarterly*
"Gravel" in *Negative Capacity*
"Digging for Colossus" in *Santa Clara Review*
"Fifty Year Stand" and "Foraging in Memory" in *Waters Deep: A Great Lakes Poetry Anthology.*
"At the Reservoir Days Before Flood Stage" in *West Texas Literary Review*

Publisher: Leah Maines
Editor: Christen Kincaid
Cover Art: Andrea L. Benson, *Unravel #1*, www.andreabenson.com
Author Photo: Benjamin Mueller
Cover Design: Elizabeth Maines McCleavy

Printed in the USA on acid-free paper.
Order online: www.finishinglinepress.com
              also available on amazon.com

Author inquiries and mail orders:
Finishing Line Press
P. O. Box 1626
Georgetown, Kentucky 40324
U. S. A.

Table of Contents

White Egret 1

I.

Colossus, PA 5
Tulip Tree 7
To Mr. ___ for Accommodating His Customers with an
    Extra Parking Lot 8
To the Laundromat Attendant and Her Husband's Missing
    Sock 9
To Fisheyes Who Collected Old Songs 10
Widow-maker 11

II.

Sirens 15
Fires on Main 16
Fifty Year Stand 18
The End of Summers 19
Gravel 21
To the Trestle Jumpers 23
At the Reservoir Days before Flood Stage 25
Digging for Colossus 27
Foraging in Memory 29

Epilogue

Upon Witnessing the Pelican's Dive 33

WHITE EGRET

I imagine the great painters of archangels
took the slender wings of egrets,
cut and lashed them to the backs of posing men.

The lake is a still life. An egret, on one leg,
watches below the surface the flutter of fish
between the subtle sway of bay grasses.

Gabriel alighting at Mary's side—
the majesty of the task—
the weight placed at her tiny feet.

I think of Icarus carrying the ambitions
of a race. The twisted maze on earth.
The father who knew too little. When

something unheard, something in this scene
hiccups, wingtips break
the surface, the egret lifts into the sky

with vast sweeping strokes. The bay
is just a bay again with two concentric circles
dissipating into the stillness.

If I could ask anything, I'd ask the egret
what it is like lifting to heaven
the weight of flesh with the weight of feathers.

I.

COLOSSUS, PA

Not much happens here
since the freight car factory
left in the 80s, though

the shift bell still rings
through the rusted
walls. There was a murder

awhile back with some
college kid and a rich
lady. Her furniture

store gutted by fire, a black
smudge on Main Street.
The insurance companies

piecing things together.
A boredom passes through
like heavy train cars

loaded with coal slag.
Mostly we ride our bikes
past the chain link fence

that keep the arthritic
machines forever lurching
in place. Goldenrod

and Queen-Anne's Lace
creep through cracks
in the concrete, wild

gardens of rubble.
Eric Madison got in
there once, and took

pictures, like something
you'd see in a fancy cafe,
far away from here—

the rust blooming through
the yellow paint, hinges
oxidized, sealed stiff,

confined to a frame.
People say he was
going places. We stop

to pitch rocks at
the metal walls,
listening for the clang

and echo, aiming
for the colossal machines,
egging them back to life.

TULIP TREE

He was stopped by a shadow of something dying.
The wings of a bat flapped in the grass

like two dog-eared pages from a book
found by a breeze. Cradling its body—

its wingspan collapsed the width of his hands—
he watched as its quiet heartbeat inside

a ribcage the size of a thimble,
before its skin-wings folded in upon itself.

He rolled it in his sweatshirt, wrapped the arms
around his waist and ran back to his house

past the eyes of his mother. He kept it
in the dark, in a shoebox under his bed

and fed it what little bugs he could find.
But it didn't eat, and the crickets chirped

 all night from inside his room.
At dawn while his parents still slept,

he lashed two sticks together and stuck the cross
at the base of his favorite tree, in May

when its orange blossoms appeared
in the high treetops, beyond the eyes of everyone

and everything, except his own
from the sill of his bedroom window.

TO MR.___ FOR ACCOMMODATING HIS CUSTOMERS WITH AN EXTRA PARKING LOT

Children
still play where dandelions once

sprouted
like freckles; where bruised

knees
now bloom with scabs.

TO THE LAUNDROMAT ATTENDANT AND HER HUSBAND'S MISSING SOCK

the woman who works
at the laundromat
is giving away her husband;

A plaid shirt one day,
Striped shorts the next,
So he'll never notice, until

He wakes one morning to
Only a sock, and a
Letter scrawled in un-

Even ink on a laundry ticket:
love is gone,
as am I. pot-roast in the fridge

TO FISHEYES WHO COLLECTED OLD SONGS

If you yell *air raid*
he'll drop
and give you twenty.

His wires they say are
all mixed up.
His eyes glazed as he reels

his way to the library
most days.
Some say he was in

Vietnam, others say
he hasn't
come back yet. I always

see him by the records
though, his
calloused factory fingers

flipping through, stopping
once every couple
albums. His big yellow

teeth beaming, smiling
as if his feet
had never left the ground.

WIDOW-MAKER

You will one day hear
your mother yelling
through the shingled wall

of your memory—
as you go spinning off
on your bike, slamming

your brakes at the ends
of alleys before the cross-
traffic can take you

with one clean swipe.
You will hear her
as you rage to the woods

where the tracks cut through,
where train cars drop
coal slag that neatly fit slingshots

aimed at birds flitting
between branches.
You will hear her voice,

clear as a dinner bell,
while you shake and shake
rotted ash snags

till the tops snap free
and fall like spears
as you flee, then return

to see what widow-makers
stand erect among
the rotting leaves.

At some point, you will
hate her, you
will think. Maybe even say it

to her face as you storm down
the stairs to hear her
yelling again, though now

with the undercurrent of a plea.
But you will go anyway.
That's what you will do.

Leave her there
at the doorway, waiting,
keeping house with your memory.

II.

SIRENS

They still talk about the '84 tornado
that came through, twisted off the tops of trees,

then scrawled its name in an erratic cursive
through cornfields. The roofless hulls of barns

still stand as relics of what's been through here.
My father remembers how they rebuilt Main Street.

How they swept the storefronts' shattered glass,
strewn like confetti, for businesses that would never

return. Some still blame the storm for that.
Tonight sirens bid us seek the nearest shelter.

My father, wordless, listens to the house listing
in its hundred-year-old frame. The rain in torrents

slams against the steep pitch of the roof, overflowing
the gutters, seeping through basement cracks.

The radio echoes off the cellar walls, assurances no
funnel clouds have touched down. Yet I know

the Norway Spruce is flailing about up there.
I can hear the porch bell, abandoned

to the winds, calling us back up. Strangely,
some small part of me hopes

those funnel clouds would
at the very least

just touch
something.

FIRES ON MAIN

We used to think whole buildings
just caught fire, the natural
end to a structure's life.

Eventually we learn
desperation oxidizes
against these gray skies,

these gray hills of steel towns,
where the railroads
lead elsewhere like track marks

for some passed over addiction;
it oxidizes like metal siding,
corrugated factory walls

of industries fled to Mexico,
just another notch
in the Rust Belt taken in.

This could be any number
of towns, really,
chock-full of bars and churches,

parishioners drowsy within,
waiting for the smell of smoke,
a whiff of salvation while

brick, slump-shouldered buildings
down Main Street reach
the ends of their lives, combust

and ascend to the insurance gods,
the necessary paperwork
denoting the dusted knob

and tube wiring—veins arcing
the length of splintering,
hand-hewn beams.

Eventually we learn what fire is.
How it both draws breath
and chokes life. The rush

to contain it. The purifying tropes
cleansing all sins.
We grow accustomed to seeing

ourselves among the rubble,
stripped all the way down,
wiping soot from our eyes, absolved,

tidying the relics among
the hollowed out
charred cavities. Sometimes

the buildings are replaced
with functional facades
the eye passes over.

Sometimes they are not—
left like cigarette burns
down Main Street.

Forgotten, either way.

FIFTY YEAR STAND

At dawn,
the big machines come
to unearth the rich,

black humus. To topple
the fifty-year stand
of red pines having grown

thick like a forest
of swaying telephone poles.
Men and women gather

to watch the first cinder-
block settle in place.
Someone says softly

bending to one ear
that *all things pass. Yes,*
comes the reply

but this is a dollar store.
Both listen
as the machines groan

and belch toward
an uncertain dusk.
The slant light leaning

upon the raw earth.

THE END OF SUMMERS

One can hear the end
of summers when
the war drums come

rattling through
the neighborhood
like a marching band

in a dry run for Friday night.
On a field nearby
 young men gather,

upon the bristling grass
as their fathers had,
in circles awaiting the bark

of their name, to collide
into one another,
under a beating sun,

until one is on the ground.
And one must be
on the ground,

because their fathers—
rubbing their arthritic knees,
sharpening their tongues

on whetting stones
passed down—lean in
expecting the echo of their names

to resound in each
body hitting the earth.
The dust rising like an offering,

to a god always hungry,
always waiting,
but never revealing himself.

GRAVEL

We didn't know
the word injustice
when we gathered

around to watch,
but we knew it was
fucked up the way

the gravel skidded
between the parked cars
at the fieldhouse

the unlooked-for
violence that ended
face down in the rocks.

Fist upon fist
pounding down. We
knew it was bad,

but we figured it
would be stopped
or punished the way

we were taught.
We didn't think
the football captain

would just peel out,
windows down, music
screaming—dust

parching our wordless
tongues, leaving us
wondering how we

should exit this scene
with Adam lying there,
gravel in his cheek

and forehead. And
on Monday, the hallways
filled with the same

clutter and cast as all
Mondays, jockeying
our way to classes.

Except Adam passing
through— pocked scabs,
gravel still buried

in his face. While
we swallow those
hard little stones

sticking in our throats
assuring ourselves that
one day, one day.

TO THE TRESTLE JUMPERS
    "And the Greenville trestle now don't seem so high."
    -Doc Watson

I thought it was about suicide
the first time I heard the song,

how there was *no work*
for the railroad man.

I imagined penniless men
teetering on the Greenville trestle high

above the Shenango.
I thought it was about my town,

with the shuttered freight car factory,
the foundries that once fed Pittsburgh.

But Doc wasn't talking about this place.
Eventually you learn

there's a Greenville in every state
and *pussy* is a word they called you

when you didn't jump,
saying the worst that could happen

were water bugs up your ass.
Yet every year someone

had to be fished out. *The Argus*
stating drugs in the system,

sometimes not. Everyone
has their reasons.

The freshman who shot herself
when I was 14, she'd be in her thirties

and still stuffed Mickey Mouses
are placed at her headstone.

She ran with that crowd
that smoked and drank

down by the river, that fed
their systems with anything

to just keep going. I can picture
her still, perpetually tanned, arms

outstretched, legs the color of August,
standing above the river,

feeling the splintering beams sway.
Maybe she needed that untethering

for an instant, a baptism
of the profane, the water

rushing over, filling in above her
to fight and kick her way back up.

We've all thought about it.
At some point we all shuffle to the edge

of the tar-pitched railroad ties.
We all know the freights

don't run here, the cops
don't give a shit. There are rocks

and slurs readied in hands
below for those that can't do it.

Eyes closed, we plug our noses,
preparing for all that's beyond our reach.

AT THE RESERVOIR DAYS BEFORE FLOOD STAGE

We lie back on the concrete drainage
having flicked all the matches

into the reservoir,
hissing at they hit the surface.

They float like compass needles
trying to deceive us.

After the Springsteen song
the radio gives us the news:

A leviathan writhing out at sea
gathering a flood at its back,

the hurricane somewhere
south of us veering inland

as you lie sunning,
dampness rising from your suit.

Everything dies baby that's a fact.
You will be gone in a week,

off to live with your father.
I watch you. Imagining

how this will go. Snakes
and hares flushing from dens.

Brown water swelling
the embankment. The reservoir

filling the woods and fields.
Hay bales torn open, the silage wrap

clinging to tree limbs, ghosts
hesitant to leave. This will never

work out. In two days it will rise over
our heads to swallow us,

but we both will be gone.
You roll onto your stomach,

the tiny hairs on the small of your back,
blonde from the August sun.

Your eyes closing. Concrete warm
against you. I can almost remember it now.

DIGGING FOR COLOSSUS

Most boys of this town grow up digging.
Rising each morning with the rusted shovels
that fit our fathers' hands, to find our way

to that remaining grassy patch in the backyard.
We say we are digging to China
(though we mean any place else),

eventually getting far enough to feel
that familiar clunk: metal on stone,
a shutter straight to the shoulders.

Then jumping down to clear the dirt,
to reveal some immutable part
of the giant stone effigy of our pasts

that lay beneath our homes, our town.
There was a time when it stood,
and all gladly worked under its shadow.

Steve found the foot once, the toenail
the length of our legs, a buried crescent moon,
his shovel striking against, wild sparks

filling the cavity. Bryan hit what seemed
the thigh or stomach and for weeks searched
with shovel blade for some crack or edge,

as if it had been a solitary rock
able to be wrenched free. This whole
town is pocked with holes. Each our own

stony end. Routes blocked by manmade
bedrock we had no hand in laying.
Nights, we collapse in our beds, turn back

to dreaming. To fill our nights with girls
we'd never touch. Words we never say.
Cities we'd never dare set foot in.

We awake again to claw at the earth
ancient grit beneath our nails
ache burning down our bodies.

FORAGING IN MEMORY

Where apple trees grow deep in the woods,
there must have been a house;
your grandfather taught you this.

You watch for where the canopy clears
and long grasses cut at your legs.
There a pair of forgotten apple trees stand,

thick with shoots splaying toward the sky,
surrounded by hemlocks and aspens
that flicker to white in wind. *Malus*

you recall him muttering. The Latin loaded
with reproach. Yet you've walked these woods,
passing through the rust-wired fences.

So you kick around the dried blades of grass
until you find the ordered row of stones,
the foundation filled in—a memory's grave.

You know the family name that owned
this land, but not why they're not here now.
Their home is by the highway, the double-wide

with faded siding where the trucks go
whipping past. Yet here the trees still bear
their heavy fruit and dip down

those highest grown. You taste one,
pocked and misshapen, still sweet despite.
Your grandfather taught you to prune:

Take the ones reaching heavenward,
leave the crooked, down-turned shoulders
for the next season's crop.

EPILOGUE

UPON WITNESSING THE PELICAN'S DIVE

Our children nod in the back seats mouthing the word *ocean*.
Meaningless to them, except for the promise of newness.

Our car winds over the ragged peninsulas, the glacial tracks,
land etched from some ancient orogeny. Moss draped pines

out one window, rocky inlets out the other. Along the way
0ur phones lose all signal. We've left that behind now.

The endless news cycles, the dailiness of life, the labyrinths
of our own making. We've escaped for now, like Icarus,

yet knowing too soon we will have to return back
to our daily blazing toward the sun. Here though,

the cabin will be quiet with dewy nights cloaked in clouds
and the day's sun burning off the morning fog.

With child eyes we'll seek riches in tide pools. Our children
will begin to know the word *ocean*—water upon the ankles

then gone, salt parching the tongue, mysteries scurrying in the wake.
Our ears will prick to some distant splash—a body falling to water—

and quietly we'll realize, it is not us, this time,
as we turn back to the rush of water over our children's feet.

www.ingramcontent.com/pod-product-compliance
Lightning Source LLC
LaVergne TN
LVHW041311080426
835510LV00009B/958